The Sound of Kindness

For Noelle & Stacey with love—*ALV*

To David, the biggest and kindest brother I have—*TM*

Books for Kids From the
American Psychological Association

Book design by Rachel Ross and Gwen Grafft
Printed by Sonic Media Solutions, Medford, NY

Library of Congress Cataloging-in-Publication Data
Names: VanDerwater, Amy Ludwig, author. | Martínez, Teresa,
    1980- illustrator.
Title: The sound of kindness / by Amy Ludwig VanDerwater ; illustrated by
    Teresa Martínez.
Description: Washington, DC : Magination Press, [2023] | Summary:
    In simple, rhyming text, illustrates how to communicate kindness.
Identifiers: LCCN 2022024103 (print) | LCCN 2022024104 (ebook) |
    ISBN 9781433841491 (hardcover) | ISBN 9781433841507 (ebook)
Subjects: CYAC: Stories in rhyme. | Kindness—Fiction. | LCGFT: Stories in
    rhyme. | Picture books.
Classification: LCC PZ8.3.V3338 So 2023 (print) | LCC PZ8.3.V3338 (ebook) |
    DDC [E]—dc23
LC record available at https://lccn.loc.gov/2022024103
LC ebook record available at https://lccn.loc.gov/2022024104

Manufactured in the United States of America
10 9 8 7 6 5 4 3 2 1

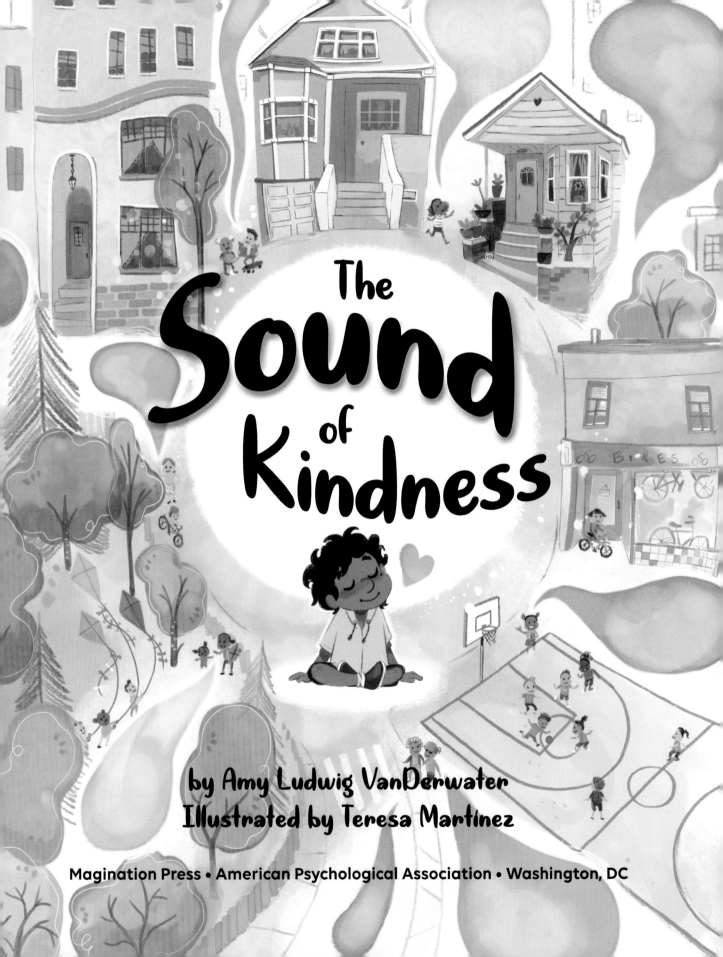

The Sound of Kindness

by Amy Ludwig VanDerwater

Illustrated by Teresa Martinez

Magination Press • American Psychological Association • Washington, DC

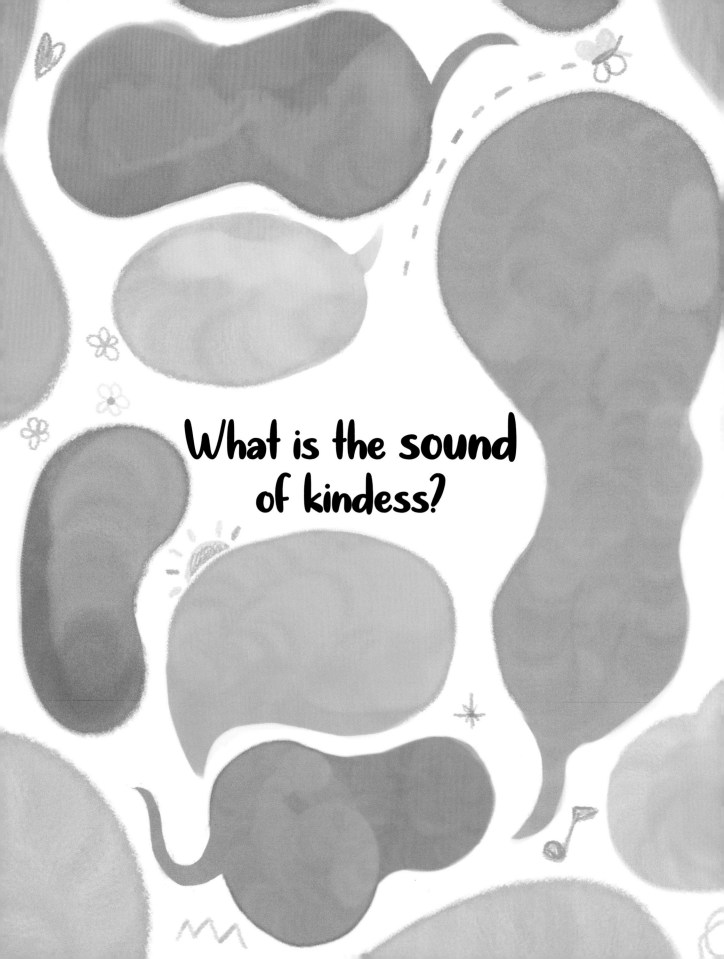

What is the sound
of kindess?

Let's take a **kindness walk.**

Let's rest a bit.

We'll work together.

I'm learning **too.**

We can **Fix** it.

We hear the sound
of kindness when we
listen to the day.

We fill our world
with kindness with the
words we choose to say.

Reader's Note

When we look for something in our world, we have a greater chance of finding it. And so it is with kindness. The adult and child in this story take a focused walk to hear the voices and sounds of kindness in their city, and they find many sincere examples. You can revisit the pages and notice with a child the many ways this book's characters are kind:

- A person helps someone else with a task or job.

- Someone eases someone else's sad feelings.

- Somebody shows joy when seeing another.

- A person gives a compliment.

- People share their belongings.

- One person encourages another to try something difficult.

- People simply enjoy their time together in gentle ways

When we think and talk about valuing kindness, we are more likely to act kind.

We can plan a kindness walk just like the adult and child do in this book, listening for examples of kindness. Such walks are a type of treasure hunt, and we can help the children in our care understand this by noticing instances of kindness together.

In this story, the characters listen for kind words, but there are many ways to notice kindness. Here are a few possibilities, but the options are endless!

Brainstorm more ideas with your child; what else can you come up with?

Quiet Kindness Walk

While this book focuses on how kindness sounds, we can also look for quiet evidence of kindness with children: the bowl of dog water outside a shop, a person holding a door, flowers in a highway median. Children will learn to notice what we notice, and we can model paying attention to quiet kindness by saying things such as:

- This small bowl of pennies here at the register is left by others for people who need them. I am grateful we could use two of them today.

- I like seeing people take the time to let their dogs meet each other. It's like the dogs become friends, and the people do too!

- Did you see that person returning the stray shopping cart to the cart holder? That may keep someone's car from getting dented on this windy day.

After you've pointed out a few examples, invite your child to share what they notice on their own.

Nature Kindness Walk

On a nature kindness walk, we simply look for beauty and tell the plants and creatures what we love about them. We can speak these thankful words out loud:

"Thank you, snow, for being so sparkly today! You make my eyes happy." Or, instead of talking, we might stop and write or draw what we appreciate in nature. This models kind feelings toward the Earth, and is a great way to practice gratitude. As we walk, we might also notice things like benches, or signs naming trees or flowers. We can talk about the kindness behind placing such objects for everyone to enjoy.

Another way to show kindness on a nature walk is to bring along a trash bag and gloves, picking up garbage and leaving the trail less littered than we found it.

Memory Kindness "Walk"

We can even go on a kindness journey without moving. Sitting together with a child, we can retell a memory of a time when someone was especially kind to us. This person may be someone we know well or someone we hardly know at all. By taking a kindness "walk" into the past, we help children understand how we change each others' lives in big and small ways through kind deeds. At fifty-two years old, I still vividly remember the woman in the blue house who placed change in my little orange Unicef box one Halloween. When I dropped a dime and couldn't find it, she hurried to give me another.

Our memory kindness walks will be more interesting to children if we tell them slowly, stretching out the details of what people said, what we saw and felt and wondered. Rather than telling a one-sentence memory, we tell our stories long so that children can feel as though they are living the stories too. Then, we can ask children to share their own kindness memories with us.

Literary Kindness Walk

We can take a kindness walk through a poem, story, or book. When reading together, we stop and note places where characters do good things for each other. So as not to lose the power of the word kind, we can use varied language that describes kindness:

- What a great friend that character is.
- This is one of my favorite parts. I love the way this character....
- I will try to be like this character. They always do what feels like the right thing.

Pretend Kindness Walk

We can go anywhere in our minds, and taking a pretend kindness walk allows us to use our imaginations, either by telling made up stories of kindness or imagining which kind things might happen in different places and situations.

- After reading a book about space, we might ask, "How might it be different to be kind inside of a space shuttle compared to inside of an apartment building?"
- "If we were as tall as skyscrapers or as strong as bulldozers, how could we use our height and strength to be kind in new ways?"

Our world and its loud news offers many angry sounds. Bringing our children on kindness walks, big and small, noticing gentleness around us, helps us to see the many ways that people lift each other up. It is not necessary to always take special kindness walks or to even name such walks in this way, but paying attention, pointing out, and celebrating the goodness of people is a gift we give our children...and too, it is a gift we give ourselves.

Amy Ludwig VanDerwater has taught writing for over 20 years, and her children's books have received accolades from the Junior Library Guild, the Society of Children's Book Writers and Illustrators, and the National Council of Teachers of English. She lives in an old farmhouse in Holland, NY. Visit amyludwigvanderwater. com and @amylvpoemfarm on Twitter and Instagram.

Teresa Martínez is a children's book illustrator who grew up in Mexico. She studied Graphic Design in Arte AC and took painting courses in Italy to learn different techniques. She currently lives in Puerto Vallarta, a small beach town full of kindness that inspires her work. Visit @teresamtzjun on Instagram.

Magination Press is the children's book imprint of the American Psychological Association. APA works to advance psychology as a science and profession and as a means of promoting health and human welfare. Magination Press books reach young readers and their parents and caregivers to make navigating life's challenges a little easier. It's the combined power of psychology and literature that makes a Magination Press book special. Visit maginationpress.org and @MaginationPress on Facebook, Twitter, Instagram, and Pinterest.